SELFTITLED

SELFTITLED

by Nicole Morning

Trident Press
Boulder, CO

Copyright © 2021 by Nicole Morning

This book is a work of fiction.

All rights reserved. No part of this book may be reproduced in any form or by any electronic or mechanical means, including information storage and retrieval systems, without permission in writing from the publisher, except for review.

ISBN: 978-1-951226-10-7

Published by Trident Press
940 Pearl Street
Boulder, CO 80302

www.tridentcafe.com/trident-press-titles

Front Cover: Detail from "The Dying Cedar" by Anne Brigman

Contents

Strategy 1
Paper James 5
Fighting Words 11
Big Window 15
Ceremony 17
One 23
Looking 27
Portrait of You at Four Years, Eleven Months,
    Fourteen Days, Nine Hours 31
Sweet Enough 37
Arrival 45
Freefall, Somehow Like Giving Birth 49
One Time 51
The Scene Inside 59
Things I Left Out 63
Seeing Stars 67
Left 81
Places I Have Lived and the Colors
    of Them 83
Self Titled 93

For my great great great great grand-mother, and her mother, who was Patience

Strategy

What're you trying to escape?
You answer, nothing.
Nothing, you insist.

& I'll buy that if we mean it in some existential way but

A scroll through history shows just how far you've
Grown away from yourself

Now I'm calling you back
Not to me, I don't mean that
You think you can't
Come back you think
Nothing can be escaped

Even infants strategize for affection
That's how long we've been playing this
Come back

I can't tell what matters more: the poem
Or the situation from which it arises
Or you reading it aloud or alone
Maybe nothing matters more
Come back

Remember making shadow stories
    on the ceiling
The sound you made when my shadow creature
Swallowed yours come back it was laughter
Come back it was mystery how my small hand
Made such a monster and we were not
Afraid come back it is you

What matters more is
How we mean it
Come back

The poem alone is nothing
Come back come back come back
The situation itself is nothing
Come back come back come back

The poem aloud
Come back
You alone
Come back

You reading the poem aloud is really something
I didn't even like the poem I loved
The way it came out of you
Like a poem come back

Like the sound you made when your small hand
Made unswallowed your shadow creature
Triumphant come back

Remember the sound your mother made
Remember the shadows of you together
Remember you were your mother
Before you knew any strategy
Before you knew escape
You knew nothing

Come back

Paper James

Paper James is five foot ten and I made him up out of parts I found inside my phone plus a few pieces I drew myself. He misspelled *quarantine* in his first message so I almost didn't reply. But he'd superliked me and when I looked at his profile again I decided his lips and his insouciant expression more than made up for the mistake. I'd been on Tinder again for about three days and somehow made about fifty matches and was in about a dozen half-assed conversations. He asked me for a book recommendation and I said *I get paid to do that*. Then I added, *jk what are you into? I'm a fantasy person*. Then I added, *I mean I'm a real person, but I like fantasy*. He said he'd been reading some heavy history about Dumas' dad or something but the chaos of the period wasn't helping his feelings about our current situation and that he's a Tolkien geek and asked for my favorite in the genre. I told him about the book I'd just finished and how it's not quite fantasy and had some heavy themes but was rendered with such light and sweetness that it was *the perfect read for this time if you like that kind of thing*. Then I didn't think of him again, so I was surprised when he replied a couple of days later and said *I ordered that book so it better be good what do I owe you n should I send on paypal or? Haha. N what's your story?* And I gave him the broad strokes and a couple days later he gave me his broad strokes and then he added, *do u feel like texting?* I typed *send ur face* and my phone number.

He sent his *face as requested*, first the *public face* and then the *pvt face*. Right away I warned him about me: how I'm fatter in real life, not into monogamy, and a writer. He said *all good I'm not looking for anything serious n you can use me for a character if u want*. He is the oldest person I've ever texted with who uses so many abbreviations. But I assume it's because his brain works so fast he doesn't have the patience to spell things out. That first night, I was pleased that he could keep up with me, I laughed out loud for the first time in a while, and the conversation ranged swiftly across my favorite subjects: books, music, the creative process, sex. Satisfyingly crass and sublime, and by one AM we had a fine repertoire of inside jokes.

Paper James is five foot ten and fits inside my phone. When he hails me from in there my vision narrows and my large unruly heart takes a small rectangular wordy shape and makes my brain light up again and again and again with the Good Feeling. My heart is phone-shaped and it fits perfectly inside the pocket of Paper James. Listen to this, read that, look what I made, isn't it strange how everyone else is so boring and same. *Fuckin n stuff is like the cherry on the sundae kissing n snugging is my shit*, he texts. The Good Feeling gets bigger until we come almost together silently in a shared rectangular space. And then we stay inside there. I send my cuddleface and he sends his cuddleface and we stay inside there until I say about my very sad thing and he thinks of ways to solve it and I say *sry it's just like in real life I always do this after, hormones I guess* and he says *it's ok* and thinks of more solutions to my sadness and we stay inside there holding each other and touching inside there somehow until I'm aroused again, just like it happens in real life and then he says *haha I got a sympathy boner too.*

Paper James is five foot ten and does not do videochat. All my girls smell something fishy and I tell him so. *What's a catfish again? Like I'm not me? I'm me.* I type *I know you're you and I LIKE U that's why I wanna hear ur voice n see u.* He is insouciant. *Send more parts pls*, I type. *Whatcha need mama?* And it's *hands* I reply like lightning. He gives me one hand and I nearly cry. I tell him I'm making a Paper James. I make him a video of myself introducing myself and showing him my favorite spooky place and send it. He says *hiiiii! Don't get abducted.* He says about his bad news and his hard day but all I can hear is how he isn't swooning even a little bit over my voice or my face or my spooky place.

Paper James is five foot ten and does not swoon. It's too early to text him and I always text first so I text my friends instead to say *I hate the way I feel waiting for him to text I just wanna text him all night and day* and then I look at his Tinder profile instead of texting him and see new pictures there, his *public face* and *pvt face*, so that smile was not just for me. I text *do u phone talk u motherfuckin catfish? Call a needy bitch.* He laughs insouciantly. I delete my

Tinder for the express purpose of not looking at his profile anymore and because I know there's no one else on there that I want to do this with again.

Paper James is five foot ten and when he puts his arms around me there is the sound of wind in tall grass, or silence.

Fighting Words

Three hours and nothing to do and the city is
    on fire.
I should've gone west but I wanted to see for
    myself.
I wanted to be something else. At least I'm not
Scrubbing the Capitol like these bootlickers
Are there are more bodies in the street now

There are bodies in the street
Bodies suspended in midair or asleep
A woman's naked ass, upside down, a live
Kitten emerging from between her erect legs
She raises her ass again and again,
    somersaulting,
Giggling in the grass of the body of the city
Breathing exhaust spraypaint piss glistening
Well-equipped bodies holding signs

I order a latte & wait in the rain
While the city's body burns
I raise my hands to the sky
I'm carrying my latte walking while
The Capitol is burning with voices
They say *WE KNOW THEY ARE SLAVE
CATCHERS WE KNOW HOW LONG*

I walk up Colfax towards your place
I'm carrying my latte alone in the rain
I've never been but you dropped a pin
I'm not going there but I'm aware
I walk in your direction wondering
Will you see me accidentally *No.*

The last thing I want is

My heart on fire but that's life
Every little cell is burning some
All of life is measured combustion
Everyone else can see me but I can't
There are bodies in the streets as usual
Pink hearts dripping at orderly intervals
Fighting words burning everywhere in the body

I'm not going to your place but
I am aware of my direction

Ever youwards   though
No.   I cannot see you

I see the bodies as I walk
I marvel at *slavecatchers*
I am carrying my latte
Knowing I'll never get as far
As your place through this
This conflagration though

I am aware

There are bodies in the streets and every one had a mother
There are bodies in the streets and somewhere is my son
I'm carrying my latte listening to the city see me

I'm a body in the street and the city is a burning body

I wonder will they fire me for saying
    fuck the police
Like I was dismissed for saying
    I'm already in love

And if that'll teach me to stop saying every stupid
Little thought that comes into my mediocre mind,
Every little feeling that crosses my hot starry heart

Strong words that mean nothing much
Brave words with no action attached.

No. I can say whatever the fuck I want

Because I'm not a poet,
Just *someone into poetry*.
I'm not a revolutionary,
I just play one on facebook.

I'm a body in the street
Carrying my latte
Ill-equipped with
Unwise words
Like love like
Our city
Burning

Big Window

Smoke makes me squint with my face angled up like this, trying to see my kitchen sink from the sidewalk. I keep the blinds open: I love the sun. I'd get butterflies watching him walk up. He held me around the hips and hid his face in my soft places like a prayer.

He texted, *jesus christ I want you.*

I texted, *read to me?*

He texted, *I'll bend you over your kitchen table and fuck you*, but it ended up being the kitchen sink. He never read me anything and I can't really see it from here, thank goodness.

Ceremony

I've been going out for groceries and to work in the empty library, that's all. Taking her for walks around the neighborhood, Netflix, stacks of storybooks, backyard gymnastics, howling out the front door at eight. The other day I found her on the porch, sitting in her carseat, staring into space. Her eyes have been looking different, tired or like she was crying even when she hasn't been. The world has grown small and it seems like the more we stay in, the harder it is to go out. But the weather is supposed to be good today and when I ask if she wants to go for a picnic her eyes light up.

We drive past the hospital where she was born and she says, *oh yeah, I remember that. I remember that, the first time I got born.* I used to panic everytime I'd pass the place but today I feel nothing. Coming up to the corner by our old apartment, I remember craving the drive-thru carwash when I was pregnant with her. Radishes, lemons, carwashes. The dark and the sounds soothed me, kinda like the ocean I guess. *Yes, I would LOVE to go in the carwash*, she says. We wait in line and I wonder if she would be this patiently excited in a normal time. I wonder when she will hug another child again. I wonder what is happening inside all of us, but especially the children. Especially my children.

This is the first time I've been in our old neighborhood in a long time and I expected to feel different. This is where I raised my son. I expected to feel *something*. Instead I drive past our old apartment and see that the raspberries I planted in another decade are still there and I feel nothing. I say, *the raspberries are still there* but she can't see them from the car and I doubt she remembers being one and braving thorns and bees to get the bright berries and eating fistfuls of them right there and we're not getting out for a closer look. My home for ten years and two children and I feel nothing about this place.

Maybe it's that the weather, while not bad, is not good. It's cloudy but it's not gonna rain.

Maybe it's sunny but mostly it's not. It's not hot and it's not cold. Not windy and not calm. The weather is nondescript, April, unwilling to commit. The trail is crowded and she goes so fast on her pink scooter that I can only keep track by her dayglo orange shirt. The shirt says *Believe In Your Dreams* in an inspiring font. I don't feel nostalgia or sadness or melancholy or joy, but I'm not depressed either. I move in the way of wood or machines just like old Emily says, but it's not like after the other great pains. It's familiar, but not. Then, those other times, I could feel the sharp living edges beneath. The bright shearing. The snap of new synapses. My wounds stitching themselves up somehow. The scars beginning to itch. Then, it was right to be still because I knew that I was healing.

Now, the pain is not behind, but before me and my feelings have arranged themselves into perfect anticipatory neutrality. I said to Patrick, *we know how to do this* and he said *and we will be erased*. Wood, quartz, lead, ice. When I touch around the leftmost part of my scar, near my hip, I might as well be touching another person. But there is no other person connected to those nerves, not me or anyone. Nothing. They are dead ends. If I move my hand further towards the scar's center I start to feel something but it's not right, like a double exposure of flesh, a fuse box where the connections are all fantastically fucked. A bad map. This is what holds me together though. Never the same as before, but I had become whole. Functional.

While she's zooming down the trail and I'm powerwalking to keep up, her dad calls. I slow down and tell him where we are and he doesn't say anything for thirty seconds while we both remember all the things we did here together but I don't feel any way about it. I ask how he is and scan his voice for signs of illness but all I hear is him remembering and regretting and wishing he was here and then she's way too far ahead so I use my mom voice to yell her name once, twice. *Did she stop?* he says. *Nope, but she heard me 'cause she's letting herself leisurely coast to a halt*, I say. He laughs and she comes barreling back towards me belting out an original tune like, *she's gonna be so mad at me! Just look at her face! Mad mad MAAAAAAD! Mom Mom MOOOOOOM!* with operatic flourish. *I wish you were here* I say, but I don't.

I packed a picnic like I promised but it doesn't seem safe to sit at the tables so we eat in the car. We don't want to go home so we keep driving. I think maybe I will see something that makes me feel something. Red Rocks, but it's closed and the snow hasn't melted and everything's fucking grey so I'm driving us home. I look back and she's asleep and there's enough space to cry so I do. This is not unfamiliar but there's a new edge to it. The classic emptiness and longing of the aging unmated woman, but now at the end of the world. I want to be looking forward to my date tomorrow but I'm not. *I used to swipe left on certain people I liked because they seemed too good for me, but I stopped doing that and now I'm going on a date with a dashing poet*, I said to my friend by way of encouragement. *But I still feel like I'm not good enough*, I added. *Good enough for what?* they asked. *Good enough for anything good*, I typed. At least we won't awkwardly wonder whether we will awkwardly kiss at the end.

I still don't want to go home and the Sheridan exit sign reminds me of Josh so I call and say we're sort of in the neighborhood. Fifteen minutes later I call again and say *put some clothes on and come outside*. And as soon as I see him I crumple up like what the fuck. What the unnatural fuck. We both make weird *want to hug you* hand motions from the required distance away. Is it better or worse that I know exactly how it feels to be wrapped up in him, the smell of his skin, the sound of his voice close in my ear? I just look and look. His eyes look the same way as my daughter's, tired or like he's been crying. I've never looked at his face for this long from this far away. I'd never noticed how pleasing is the shape of his eyes, how it's the heaviness of his eyelids that make him seem so warm and sexy even if you don't know him, the crinkly sweetness around them from all his smiles. He's working at not one but two shelters and his girlfriend is a nurse. They don't touch each other either.

Last time I talked to Nick he helpfully pointed out that *people you know are gonna die* and so this formal feeling. How long will it take for the children to forget that hugging is dangerous? We are always all going to die and never know for sure *when* but now we know there are x dead and that we will definitely see someone we love for the last time soon or maybe we already have and there will be no funeral or if there is we will likely go to it alone so my *Nerves sit ceremonious, like Tombs--*

One

I'm up late doing the math on my next steps. Calculating and figuring on equations I don't have the skills or necessary fucking values to begin to solve. It's the kind of math I've been doing for almost 24 years, but usually with less death. These days, I can't even formulate most of the problems. There's just a series of variables dancing some kind of postmodern ballet in my brain. So I switch to the man's face, a numberless place. I think of kissing the man's forehead. I think of touching the man's temple with my lips. The knot of the man's jaw, I would whisper there. But kissing the man is one of the factors, though tangential, and before I know it, I'm back in the problem. There are two kinds of death rates. There are numbers of new cases today. There is my hourly rate of pay.

There is the number of hours I have childcare, provided by the grandparents. There is the percentage of risk of serious illness based on age. There is the number of days that school may or may not be held, starting one month from today. There is the number of days since my child has hugged another child. There is the number of times I can race up the wall against her, how many people in the playground, how many are wearing masks, how many more 90+ degree days we will be having. The man's sweat on my lips. The cost of daycare, the income limits for the daycare subsidy, the income requirements for an apartment rental. I do a mortgage calculator, just for the fuck of it. With my income, I can afford to buy a $45,800 home--here is a real number, a known value.

    I think I could be ok and fine in this situation, sharing a bedroom with my daughter in my parent's home not touching men or hugging friends or going to the museum or ever being alone and not knowing where is my son indefinitely but not forever if I just read novels and write poems and send people beautiful things in the mail and videocall Dean and email Susie and get an air conditioner and try harder at playing pretend and do more yoga in the study where if I stand right in the center of it I can fit without hitting any furniture with my long limbs. And then I imagine the mail handler getting sick just so I could send something beautiful. And I think of my girl not playing with other children indefinitely but not forever. I think of dying and how I've always wanted to and it's forever been the thought of someone else raising them that's made me live. I think I don't want to die. I think of all the plans I made that didn't work out that way. I think of my son but not too hard. I do not count the days since he sent word or how many until his birthday nor allow myself to consider how I might celebrate it this year. I think of how yesterday when I asked the parents for their thoughts re: some parts of all these motherfucking equations, stepmother said, I *could* say this is not my responsibility to solve. And how the rage that sits right beneath my heart pulsed like a snake then.

 I, of all people, know this. Since I was fifteen, my life has been these equations. Stepmother or no one needs ever to remind me that I *alone* am responsible for doing this math--and now *there* is the realest number of all, and at least something to count on.

Looking

when i was twenty i told thomas kennedy that
 bob dylan sucks
so next time i saw him he took my walkman
 out of my hands
put *the freewheelin'* in and pointed for me to sit.
 just listen,
he said, pre-exasperated with the argument on
 my face.
so i sat in the sun and watched everyone walk
 the plaza
while he sang me all their stories, the whole
 human story.

i guess my son was with my mom or school or
 somewhere
then i got drunk or read to him or cried us both
 to sleep

and that's how the first half of my twenties
    went, mostly.

twenty years later i learn there are hard
limits to what love can do and that
in oklahoma city there is no place to be
both out of the wind and in the sun.

i know how tired you get just trying to take
a shit or have a thought in private always
cold walking always to eat to sleep in
peace making yourself invisible so

i'm sorry to bother you
but i'm looking for my son i wonder
have you seen him

and at this point i sound like a reasonable
person but i hold the photos out at a weird
angle as though showing the face of a sleeping
newborn or a rare manuscript, close enough
you can get a good look but fearful, clutching.
i watch your face. sometimes you look right
through but usually you look at his face
then you look at me then you say,
how long's he been missing?

while my brain tries to answer my face breaks
   like thin ice on a lake and some inhuman
voice says it says how long says how impossibly
   long my baby has been gone from me
says all my worst nightmares says *if you do see
   him just tell him call his mama. please.*

i want to say, *and please call your mama too* but i
don't because i know some mothers are monsters maybe that's why you are standing sitting
sleeping walking pissing living here invisible in
the wind not home. so i say silently *i see you are
someone's child too i'm sorry there is no place safe for
you i'm sorry i have nothing to give i'm sorry there
are so many monsters but i see you have grown strong*
while i'm looking in your beautiful eyes and out
loud you, strangers all across the city, you say
to me

i'm so sorry
i'll pray for y'all
i wish i could help
i hope you find him
i really hope you find him
i wish i could ease your pain
everyone wants to be found someway

i fold the pictures back up into my pocket
i say *thank you for taking the time to look*

i fold the pictures back up into my pocket
over and over until the paper is soft cursing
my ignorance cursing the city cursing the wind

cursing every minute i ever spent
lost not looking at my child
with love on my face

Portrait of You at Four Years, Eleven Months, Fourteen Days, Nine Hours

You're lying in my arms, across my lap, like a baby. Pink cat eye sunglasses perched on your head. Unusually docile in the rainy summer evening, recovering in my arms after a bad fall. That's why I have time to notice your toes. Your toes are exactly the same shape as every time I ever held you, but now they are so big and stretched out far away at the end of your long girl legs, spilling out over my lap onto the chair's arm. They fall at exactly the same angle as always, dirt between your toes as usual, a ragged square of silver nail polish on the big toe. You painted them yourself. I remember the time I wore you to a poetry reading, before you'd taken your first steps. Snug against my heart in a pale green wrap, your plump baby legs and bare feet dangling out, dancing near my belly and a woman asked if she could touch them, a clean miniature version of these feet before me now. *So pristine*, she said. *So tiny*. She stroked your little soles, barely bigger than a thumb, and you smiled at her. Your toes are for twirling, transporting you to ever greater heights, and that's how you fell.

The scar on your right ankle has stretched with the rest of you, thinner now, so much smaller than it seemed on your newborn body. It looks like a sign from an alien alphabet, ghostly dots and lines. Your left ankle is newly skinned and bruised. Your right knee has an old dark scab. Last night you webbed your fingers around that knee like a wizard, without touching the scab and screwed up your face to say *I WANT TO SCRATCH IT GRRRR*. Your long legs are decorated with fading magic marker, mostly diagonal lines and X's in pink and green. The marks are faint and shadowy, just like the baby plumpness of your body.

You're wearing a two piece swimsuit, each piece from a different set. The top is layers of red, white and blue, with stars. The bottom is neon green and yellow, with tiny pink ruffles, faded from washing. Every day you wear some variation of these items: the two swimsuit sets, a gymnastic suit, a black leotard, a pink leotard, black tights, pink tights. You want to sleep in these outfits and sometimes I let you. Yesterday before work, I snapped at you over your insistence on wearing the black leotard over the pink tights. They were filthy but you wanted to wear them. You covered your ears and hunched your shoulders when I said, *No! They're not clean. You can't always do everything you want to do!* And before I left I said I was sorry but you just looked away.

    Now there are new scrapes too on your shoulders beneath the swimsuit straps. Your hair falls halfway down your back and in your face, almost golden but not quite, straight, *long like Rapunzel*. No, you don't want me to put it up, you like it *down*. It's just like your father's. And the lines of your body are, too: long and strong and imbued with visibly solid agility. We called him on the laptop earlier and he watched you draw a smiling mermaid with a giant head. His eyes lit up as he saw you mark out each tiny scale of her fish tail so meticulously. His face usually fills up the screen but when he leans back you can see what's behind him and I don't know if you wonder because you never ask anymore where he is and I don't say the word.

I ask does it still hurt and you say *no*. I say *we gotta be careful about bumps on the head because* and you interrupt to say *you could get a concussion* and then you go on to explain. You learned it from one of your favorite shows: twin doctors teaching about the body. You want to go to London so you can meet them. I brush the hair out of your eyes and for once you let me. It was an epic fall and so you are letting me hold you.

Your hands, too, same shape as they've always been but so much bigger hanging on the ends of this tall girl body. Last week's scrapes healing on your palm, ten different shades of nail polish, worn away so I can see the dirt beneath your fingernails. I can see three faint freckles on your nose, plus the real one above your lip. Your mouth is always moving, always opening to let out song, rhyme, big weird thoughts. So much to say and such a big voice to say it with. For the first two weeks of your life you were silent, but when you finally cried what you said was power. Your father is there in all the lines and shapes of your body except your eyes. Those are shaped like mine, but a color all your own: grey or silver or green or blue, always flashing, changing, moving like you. Some impossible color like the ocean.

Girl, you love an adventure. Gardening bores you and flowers too, but you'll hunt bugs and berries and boast about how *my mom planted all this*. You'll taste anything from the garden, even the bitter herbs. This morning you woke up smiling, like every morning for the last four years, ten months, fourteen days. Every day of your life that your face was free to smile, you have woken up that way. With a smile and a *great idea*.

You were trying to do some elaborate trick in the mismatched swimsuit and pink sunglasses. Some elaborate trick involving a very large exercise ball and a jump and a climb and a twirl and you fell. Sometimes you still reach inside my shirt looking for comfort, but not today. This time last year you drank the last drop of my milk. Now, you just let me hold you. You're quiet, for once. Maybe you're thinking about how hard the world can be or how soft I am, how strange it is to be in a body that bruises and bleeds and breaks and leaps and sings, or maybe planning your next elaborate trick or only looking at the rain but you don't say and I just hold you, magnificent.

Sweet Enough

My throat hurts and I'm shivering a little and I'm trying to figure out why. Of course it started on Tinder, some time ago. Several weeks or more. My first time around. Tinder, text, videochat, online chess, he calls me when I say I'm sad, sends me terribly unflattering selfies, makes me laugh, tells me good stories and hopes I have nice days.

He says he likes how diligent I am about making sure he's not a murderer, by getting to know him and insisting we meet in public. I like that he uses words like diligent. When he finally comes to town, the best I can do is one hour between dropping off the kid at daycare and the start of class. So we meet for coffee and it's the earliest date either of us has ever been on. It's colder than it should be and snowing.

He's better-looking in person than in photos and by the way he's looking at me, it feels like he thinks I'm better-looking in photos than in person and it seems like he wants to leave. We talk about things. He leans back in his chair, looking half-interested, some kind of insolent/angry grin/frown on his face. My glasses fog up. I look down and away. My hands go to cover my face. My arms cross over my belly and my shoulders curl down over my heart. I feel this happen and resist, square my shoulders, raise my head, reach for tobacco so my hands have something to do. I say *I'm nervous*. He says *don't be*. I don't know what things we talk about but we carry on even though it looks like he wants to leave. I ask if he wants to walk me to class and he does, against the wind and snow and we go for a hug outside the classroom and he reaches inside my coat to pull me close and it's sweet and warm against the wind and snow.

Sweet enough to make me wanna walk out of class all morning and I almost do. He wants to cancel the morning and cuddle too. I stay in class but I text a friend to ask if she can babysit for a couple of hours that night. It's a go. I'm not sure he's not a murderer but I remember that Ted Bundy's or someone's wife was married to the dude for years and never suspected so. I send my bestie a picture of his face, his name, the room number, and a final selfie in case of murder and she encourages me to have fun and not die.

I go in the room and though we've been texting about cuddling and such all day, I'm not brave now that I'm here and he's there and we're on the bed, in cuddle range but still. Separate. I say *I'm nervous*. He says *I'm not*. But I'm more nervous than I expected and I think it's because he's nervous but pretending not to be, just like this morning. I always feel the way other people around me feel but also how I feel and sometimes it's hard to distinguish which are my feelings, other people's feelings, or my feelings inspired by other people's feelings.

We tell each other about the times we almost got murdered, respectively. We try getting close from a few different angles, but he makes himself somehow hard to approach. He looks that same way as on our first date this morning, half-amused, half-indifferent, half-angry. Finally I turn my back and he curls himself around me and a cuddle is achieved. And he touches my face and his hands are sweaty and I realize yes. He's nervous. And I like the way he's touching me, and I like that he's nervous, and I like the way he looks standing at the edge of the bed looking at me and I like the way his head feels in my hands and I like how he smells and I like the way he keeps touching my face. As though he finds it beautiful.

Afterwards, I don't feel nervous and once I'm dressed, I walk right up and kiss him goodbye with confidence. I want to see him again and all week he says he's coming back every day but he doesn't. By the time he does come I'm already mad. We've already texted about the things we like to do and have done to us and we like the same things and they are not sweet. I text *can i stay with you* and he replies *for sure*. I say *i mean sleep with you* and he says *I knew what you meant*. It's colder than it should be and late. I go into the room and I'm nervous. He's not. For real this time, he's not nervous, and he is easy to approach and I do a good job and then we're relaxed and happy and we talk. He touches my foot in a casual familiar way. He grins with childish glee, telling me about things he likes and touching me gently and it is sweet.

And he kisses me and by now he already knows where to bite my neck to make me squirm and how hard but I push him away and shake my head at him and say *no marks i gotta be professional tomorrow* and he agrees not to leave any that can be seen and he is careful with his hands and his teeth on my neck but only there. His hands around my little throat, my little hands around his throat. And we get closer than you can with sweetness sometimes and I try to sleep but he doesn't let me and I love it and finally at five AM I have to leave but first we are fucking just once more and he's far away but I pull him close so all his weight is on me and my face is right up against his neck and his face and his freckles and his scent and his sweat and I wrap my arms around his shoulders and his head that I love the shape of and we are close. Close, close, in motion and it is sweet.

Sweet enough I can't stop thinking about it all next day and careful as he was, still my neck aches though there are no marks visible above the collar of my professional clothes though there is a bruise on my thigh there is a bruise just below my collarbone there is a bruise on my other thigh there is a bruise everywhere where his hands or his teeth were and I keep pressing on this bruise or that as I am being professional and it is sweet and we text how we can't wait to meet this way again and then.

He's coming but he doesn't. He calls but accidentally. Leaves a voicemail but not on purpose. I listen to it over and over trying to suss out the situation and fear frissons strangely through my belly and up into my heart. What is the situation. This much fear is strange to feel because. It's not like. We're anything. But his voice reminds me of this or that man and I want the sweetness and the notdying some more. I press on this or that bruise and the sweetness follows the fear through me and threads more fear behind it and it's fine we're not even anything.

I call and he doesn't answer. I text and no reply. It's fine. I don't care what the situation is because it doesn't concern me and I'm not gonna bother myself with this bullshit and the next morning I spend extra time putting on eyeshadow and an outfit and perfume that is extra pleasing to me and I have the bruises and that's enough and I am driving fast through the city blasting *...Like Clockwork* smelling myself being beautiful alone and alive and then. He texts me his room number and I go there because I want him to smell me and I want more of him even though the situation is increasingly obviously unwholesome though it doesn't concern me.

I go into the room and start taking off my shoes and I say *quit being so fucking shady* and he says *i'm not*. I climb into the bed and he doesn't look at me or smell me or say anything and I don't know what to do, I don't know how to get close to him but that's what we want. I put myself by his side and smell him and try to look in his eyes and say *hi*. I want to ask him what's wrong but I know he won't say anything so I don't bother. We fuck but he won't come close and it's not sweet or anything at all and I don't know what to do. I turn my back and he curls around me and puts his arm across me, close to my throat. I stay for a minute then say *I'm gonna go*. He says *no* and tightens his arm against my leaving and it is sweet. Soon we are fucking again but it's nothing at all. I start getting dressed. I rebraid my hair in front of the mirror and say, *I'm definitely putting you in a tinder story. Do you want to know what I'm going to call it?* He says *yes*. I can see him in the mirror out of the corner of my eye. I say, *deathwishes*, but I can't see what he thinks about this because his face is blank and I'm looking in the mirror.

Then I'm tying my shoes and I think about rolling a cigarette before I go but I know that's only because I want to prolong my stay, give him more time to say or do something sweet but I know he won't and I want to kiss him but I know he'll turn away so I don't. I stand up and say *goodbye* with confidence.

I'm only angry at myself for going there at all. He texts me in the afternoon. I wonder why. I reply. I wonder why. I type, *you're indifferent*. He replies, *not all the time*. I write, *it's fine we all have limited fucks to give*. He replies, *I give fucks about you, I'm just kinda going through a lot*.

I say, though I know he won't answer, so why, I type, *what's going on?* He doesn't reply. I say, though I know I shouldn't bother, I type, *i want to be ur friend as well as fuck you so if u wanna talk or i can help...* No reply. So I listen to the voicemail again, wondering what is the situation, wondering how I can help, wondering why the sweetness is not sweet enough to inspire him to reply. I puzzle over the pieces, I wonder what he's thinking, I wonder if there is nothing behind the indifference. What is the situation. I think of how it felt at 5 AM to be that close and then I notice I'm cold and my fists are clenched and my throat hurts and I realize it's only from trying not to cry over nothing.

Arrival

I mailed the thing and then

I promised myself never to write about being in love again. As a topic, it's tired. As a pursuit, it's vain. As a feeling, also tired.

It's just that I ordered your book from Amazon some time ago. I couldn't have you so I thought, fine I'll buy the books. It felt like cheating because Amazon sucks but also because I wanted you to give it to me. The book. Anyways. I fell asleep facedown on my bed like five hours after I got up this morning because there is no other escape and it's very tiresome being this way but upon awakening in the early evening because the dogs were barking because the mail came my face hurt and everything felt worse. Anyways. I went to smoke a cigarette with my face hurting and my heart weird from sleeping with my sadness in such a position and there was the mail, stuck in the slot, balanced about three quarters in this side. I knew it was your book because everything else had already arrived. The cardstock, the socks, the wooden beads, your other book, another book, the body butter, whatever. The goods. All the goods had arrived so I knew this newly arrived arrival must be your book. There was nothing else it could be and even though I ordered it very long ago, I remembered it was coming. Anyways I sat down on the step by the mail slot with my cigarette smoking and my face hurting and my heart weird and I open the package and it's your book in shrinkwrap and I consider just leaving it inside the shrinkwrap to prove something but I can't understand what so I start pulling at the seams but i can't get a grip or find an opening and I wonder if the universe is urging me to prove something by leaving the shrinkwrap on and then I'm really determined to get this fucker open anyways i go

Fumbling on, finally find an opening or rather a tear, I make one, I have to create the opening and then i've got this fucker open, proving to the universe who's in charge here and that there's nothing that could be proved by me leaving this shrinkwrap on that's stupid why I would even think of such a thing I bought it anyways so this book of yours with such a nice shape and color and size and font and overall holy fuck because

There inside it is an inscription from you

Ending in XOXO

Like maybe if I actually clutched my heart I would say, ok, this is something I learned from TV but I don't. I just want to clutch my fucking heart and throw up it feels sooooo something did you sign them all what the fuck

The book itself is bad enough (I mean it's really good, just, already hurting me by being your book) but this goddamn inscription

And this is fine if across town your mail comes and you see my handwriting on it and you want to clutch your fucking heart

It's fine if you don't I mean I didn't but I do need you at least to want to at the sight of my handwriting inside my book that came in your mail today

Free fall, somehow like giving birth

Every time the phone rings I think it's you.
I never think it's them calling with bad news.
It's usually about my extended warranty.

I take a little taste of someone else's grief
Just to get away for a while.

I wanna throw my fucking phone in the ocean
But it's too far and then you couldn't call.

The men place a consoling hand on my shoulder or thigh. The gesture is patient, empty. I hate them all.

I never *think* it's bad news but my heart does something every fucking time the fucking phone rings, something that makes me tired, shakes me, hollowing me out slow,

No news

They say
No news is

Not knowing how this kind of no news is inside me

No news is
No news

No news is
Nothing to let go of

No news is an ocean of the day you were born

No news is exactly like the words I don't have

Saltwater, bloodred, you in the world

One Time

My son's kindergarten year we lived in one half of a white duplex with orange trim, catty-corner to a Carnegie library, four blocks from the elementary school. Red carpet in the bathroom, black mold on the walls, silver foil in the closet. I never had a proper crack pipe, I just smoked it in rolled up foil and for some reason I was afraid to throw the foil away so I kept collecting it in a box. Rent was $225 a month but I rarely paid. Jimmy Ray would come to collect and I'd just be like, *eeee but I don't even have any cash til next week. You wanna smoke a bowl?* And we'd get stoned and he'd grin and stare at me and then he'd leave as though he'd forgotten why he'd come. It was four rooms in a straight line with doorways between. Living room, kitchen, bedroom, bathroom. And the closet.

I never even smoked that much crack because I was always getting ripped off because I didn't know anything about drugs and I thought we were all friends. We *were* friends. Sort of. Before the duplex was a big apartment, also white but with blue trim and a big covered porch that looked out over the biggest nicest park in town. I was engaged to a big decent German guy I'd met in Intro to Philosophy and the three of us lived there. We'd been going steady for a couple years and my kid was calling him dad and he proposed and I said yes even tho I felt a certain hollowness and obligation. He'd quit grad school because it required too much creativity and critical thinking. It was too self-directed, he said. He had thought there would be more structure. So he turned his ambitions to retail and by the time I moved out he was store manager. Before we moved I'd already broken up with him and begun fucking other people. In our bed while he was at work. In our driveway while he slept. He cried and tore his hair and beat his chest and I felt nothing but a flash of pity and an urgent desire to be away. Eventually he moved up from store to district to regional manager and now he lives in a big white house overlooking a golf course.

So finally I moved me and the kid out into the orange-red-black-silver place. Mostly I was fucking in a certain circle of skaters. We'd be hanging out smoking weed at one guy's grandma's house all the time and I was always the only girl. They'd all disappear into the kitchen and one time I followed and asked what they were doing and why were they leaving me out. I said *just let me this one time then don't ever let me again*. Within a few months I was skinnier than I'd been since I was a child. My mom asked how I was losing weight and I said *I'm on the Jenny Crack diet* and laughed reassuringly at the utter impossibility of the idea of me on crack. Later, Billy said then I looked like a bobble head doll with my big head on such a skinny neck. Later, I learned Billy had told half the town he'd fuck them up if they sold me drugs.

I was waitressing and I guess I was working at Subway, too, because I remember feeding my boy grilled tomato and cheese sandwiches made with a big block of sliced white American Subway cheese and throwaway ends of Subway tomatoes. I remember dropping the cheese and cutting off the part that had hit the floor and bringing the rest home. I remember slicing the tomatoes in the machine and picking out the ends, like we were supposed to, and saving them to bring home instead of throwing them away. I remember spending my tips each day on crack or coke and then I'd cook it, but no one tipped at Subway, so I guess I had two jobs then but still never had rent money or food money though I always had weed, which made it a little easier to comedown.

That first time, I was still living with Mr. Store Manager and I remember going home after and lying in bed with my back to him and hurting like a black hole where my heart was. More. More. More. But there was no more and feeling that way is something you can't unfeel. I mean you feel better eventually but you never forget that it is possible to feel that bad, and that alone changes you.

Ruby lived around the block from the duplex in a big old grey house with little old Bobby. She wasn't much older than me, maybe 22 or 23 but Bobby was like 50 and he had the blackest meanest eyes I've ever seen and everyone knew he beat her and that her husband would be getting out of prison eventually. Bobby always made me think of Rumpelstiltskin, in a version where the creature plans to eat the bargained child. I don't know how I knew them, probably one of the skater boys took me there to score sometime. Ruby and Bobby would erupt into violent arguments often and one time the yelling turned to blows and wrestling and Ruby got the upper hand and suddenly she was straddling his head, violently rubbing her crotch on his nose and mouth and then they were laughing at the look on my face. Ruby had a baby once in a while and one time she left him with me at my place and he wouldn't stop crying and I thought it must be because he must be a crack baby but then she came back and laughed at the look on my face and said *he don't like the blanket on him like that* and took it off and he stopped crying. One time she came by to use my shower and she left the door open and I saw her standing naked in the tub wet with all her bruises and curls and curves and then she stepped out dripping onto the thick red carpet, laughing at the look on my face. Ruby took me to some other old dude's house one time and he had a proper crack pipe and I hit it and hit it and then we all drove to some other house and then they were gone and I was in a bedroom with a stranger and on the nightstand were little portions of crack, many glorious little mountains lined up and I asked for some and he asked if I wanted to fuck and I knelt at the foot of the bed and he lifted my skirt and folded me over facedown and I stared at the nightstand and then there was another stranger waiting for me in another bedroom but I walked out the front door instead. I was wearing a bright red spaghetti strap tank top and a long grey cotton skirt with a spiral I'd handprinted near the hem and it was cold. Two girls picked me up and asked me where I was going and I said I didn't know. They laughed at the look on my face and said *dressed like that guera, chuh, what did you think was gonna happen?* and shook their heads and dropped me off at Allsups. Shortly after Ruby's husband got out of prison he ran her over with a car and she died of it.

Are you also wondering where my kindergartner was in all this? Your guess is as good as mine. I don't remember ever going into the library kittycorner from our place, but sometimes we'd sit outside it in the grass. I'd spread a blanket out and tell him to go play and I'd smoke a joint and watch him turn somersaults. One time I walked him to school in the morning and the teacher reminded me about the cupcakes I was supposed to bring that afternoon so I went home and started baking them and one of the skater boys knocked on the door and handed me a little rock he owed me and I tried to wait but I smoked it right away and then I carried the cupcakes into kindergarten with a black hole where my heart was.

One time I stayed up three days and three nights painting a giant hand on the living room wall, the side without the mold. Floor to ceiling, in blues and reds and blacks and purples, and in the center of the massive palm I painted MOLE RUIT SUA. Now when I see that hand in my memory, I see that it is the universal gesture of *stop* and the nearly universal symbol of protection, minus the eye. But I wasn't thinking anything of the sort at the time. One time I took a picture of my son in the living room, in his school uniform, making a funny face. And there is the hand behind him. When we'd cross the street he'd hold up his own little hand with authority, palm out, confident but a little afraid, telling the oncoming traffic to stop.

He always had trouble falling asleep and I would lay there on my back beside him fighting an urgent desire to be away and just when I thought he'd fallen asleep and I was about to rise and be away, I remember that he would wriggle his little hand underneath my neck to make sure I was still there and then I'd stay a little longer, listening to him breathe.

The Scene Inside

Living room, they're arguing again then

His eyes go hard and his eyes go black
And it's his eyes. Not his, his and it is
An eye in the center of a woman
An eye in the center of a woman

One eye is closed
One eye is closed

His eyes are half closed, he's tired he says
Half closed like he can't stand to look
Half closed like it's not worth the
Effort the man is
Away

The two eyes are closed, the woman
Measures herself against a tree perhaps she

One eye is open
One eye is open

She watches herself fall
It's a lot like flying she
Smiles towards the earth
She's done this before
She's calling his name
She's fighting the trees
Embrace she's not a body
She's the earth itself facedown
It's a lot like flying calling
His name, it's an aerial

An aerial shot, there, just like in the movies
The camera spirals up and out it's a film
It's almost flying she and we see the body
Woman's body the body of a woman a body

There, facedown

It's just that the color she's wearing is very
Hard to describe but makes her easy to see
There on the floor of the forest the body
On the forest floor, an aerial view, red.

But not quite. Not bloodred. And the threads

Of the eye, the threads holding the black eye in the woman's almost red center, those threads are bluest blue. Holy mother blue. The eye is misshapen, black, the crooked blue she stitched herself, eye to center the eye is open, pressing itself to the earth she's calling his name towards the sky he's away she's spinning exactly like the earth away

The eye is open to the sky she lies on her back
The woman is straight out of St Vincent Millay

From her place facedown in the forest

She says

and inside

Our living room
Scent of pine
Thread of blue
Aerial view

She says
And says

And says
From facedown in the forest
Into the living room she says

what you deserve

Things I Left Out

How he sat with her and supervised her toenail painting, played pretend restaurant and laughed at all the hilarious shit she was saying while I cooked dinner. How I rarely cook because it's too hard because the dishes are always dirty. How I listened intently from the kitchen laughing and crying quietly because the hilarious shit she says is funnier when there's someone else around to hear it.

How when hell broke loose the texts were flying like, *enjoy jail calls from the hole, slut*,
and *I hate you and wanna fuck you*
and *bitch i hate you but i do wanna be lil spoon*
and *you're the bitch*
and *you don't get to call me a piece of shit and expect me to make the sauce*

and *fine you can come if you keep ur stupid mouth shut*

SHUT. Unless you are eating my pussy
and *I'm telling you if you give me 5 you'll understand* so I gave him five and I didn't say a word while he explained how he fucks everything up, he's an accomplished *self-saboteur*, I listened to it all again for five full minutes. Then he looked at me and said, *whatever my best situation is, I fuck it up. And right now. You're my best situation.*

How while I was cooking and laughing and crying I was thinking again about how I was well into my 20s before I realized that what I thought was *man smell* was actually *man who'd been drinking smell* and that right now she can smell the whiskey as well as I can and how

She kept calling him the name of the last guy who was my friend even though that other guy was never around while she was awake and then as I'm writing this, her dad calls from the hole and I say *shit* as I knock over her milk and she says *shit* and he says *rabbit, don't cry over spilled milk* and how

This morning after we brushed our teeth she insisted my extra toothbrush in the cup was Nick's and then arranged the three of them into conversation and how I am so angry almost all the time and how

Strange that Nick's mom was 15 when she had him just like I was 15 when I had my son and how my heart cannot compute the feeling of him missing for months hating me and how my sister said *it's your fault he's so messed up from the way he was raised, just leave him alone* and how exactly around the time

When my son turned four I started drowning in my own poetry and cocaine and fucking and I started not being able to stand how much he needed me just like I can't stand how much she needs me now that she is four why when they were babies it was fine but there's something about being four that is intolerable to me how I can't stand not being able to stand them needing me when they are the reason I still exist they are the best I ever tried how it feels always like drowning and failing always at everything and poetry & fucking & parenting will tear me

apart if I have to keep doing it alone yet this is
all I want and this is all I am and maybe it's how

I was four once
I needed something
Whatever happened
No one could stand it

My small center collapsed

And maybe
This is the source of poetry
And maybe
This is the gravity holding me to him.

Seeing Stars

The man is built for violence. His body says so, in all caps. Our bodies are full of signs and he starts reading mine after he invites me inside. We're sitting on his couch and he's touching my arm and reading the pictures there. He's about to ask what tattoos I have besides those then he says, *nevermind, I'm gonna see them all in a minute*. And he smiles a wonderful smile. One that shows his teeth. Up until now I've been wondering if I got him wrong and worrying that maybe I'm not gonna get fucked after all. Because he's been entirely circumspect until now.

He's super clean and he smells so good but I can barely catch his real scent. Besides the Magic Hour with The Poet, this is the closest I've been to a man in six months. And he's fine as fuck. His beard is big and dark, but neat and threaded with silver, just the way I like. His black hoody has come off and he's sitting next to me on the couch, his t-shirt tight over his big tattoed chest and biceps. Those big arms and shoulders are the reason I chose him. I love those kind of curves and I know how hard they work for them. Outside he was so circumspect I kept expecting him to call me *ma'am*. We stood by the river and talked about our jobs, our families, laziness, the internalized shame of growing up poor. Standard first date conversation, though we were both aware it's also our last.

His voice is deep and his teeth are sharp and he's kissing me now on the couch. It's easy. I'm not nervous. Usually I give some disclaimer before a new hookup, like, *fatter in person* or *my body is not that great*, but for some reason I didn't this time. I guess because neither of us is from here and I know I'll never see him again; I've got nothing to lose and I chose him not just because he was nearby and he's got a hot body. It's that his hot body happens to be the same size and shape as that of The Man Who Will Not See Me. I'm trying to both achieve and erase something by fucking this guy, so part of me doesn't really give a fuck what he thinks of me. Also though, I want to give him something. I want to spend some affection on him. This morning, after we'd agreed on an evening date, I spent a long while thinking about his body and what I wanted. I wanted to worship.

Now, I want to kneel before him but he pulls me onto the bed and most of his clothes are off and though I want to take my time kissing those shoulders and those arms, that glorious chest, I'm already pulling at his waistband. There's a scar there and I pause to trace it. *What's this?* He smiles in a strange way and says, *that's a big scar.* I know how it can be with scars so I move on. Now I can smell his real scent and I go delirious. I can't take my time at all.

He thrusts inside me and puts one hand around my throat in the same motion. I wonder what it is about me that asks to be choked because I never *ask* for it but they always do. Maybe it's just something people do these days, nothing personal. Perhaps a little light choking is standard fare these days.

He says *shhhh* close in my ear and when I don't shhhh he puts his hand over my mouth. *Be quiet*, he says. *Be quiet, you little slut*, he says close in my ear, and he fucks me harder. He keeps his voice close in my ear and his hand over my mouth or around my throat and he's hurting me and I like it. It doesn't take much to hurt me. I am soft. I'm a big woman but I'm small inside and it doesn't take much to hurt me and he's a big man. He whispers how he wants to cum all over me and then he does.

Before I can even enjoy the sweetness of it he's standing up and reaching for a towel and he's circumspect again. He doesn't clean me up, he hands me the towel. Maybe this is the difference between casual sex and true intimacy: who wipes away the cum and how carefully. I can remember someone doing this, gently washing me with a warm cloth in the afterglow, but I can't remember who so I must've had my eyes closed. I can't think of anyone who would've touched my soft belly so tenderly, but the memory is there.

I ask about his scar and he tells me the story. He stretches out beside me but not close enough to cuddle. I want to. I want my whole body close against his whole body that is so like someone else's. I ask about his ex-wife. I'm touching his big arm and I ask *is this ok?* It's ok but there's a big burn on his back, an accident from yesterday. The charred skin has peeled away in one spot and there's raw flesh there.

You want me to clean that? Nope.

I think we're done but I wanna touch him some more so I say, *I wish I would've spent more time sucking your beautiful dick*, and he flips over into his back and says, *well go right ahead*. And I do and we're fucking again and this time we say it: *I want you to hurt me. I want to hurt you*. And I'm wondering *what the fuck*. Why is this so?

I go back to Jade's, videocall Dean and tell them (mostly) all about it, reveling in the intimacy of friendship and the relief of getting fucked. I'm going to write a story about male vulnerability and violence. All the pieces are swirling in my head: the Poet's *no*, the tinder's scar and the raw flesh beneath his new wound, the curves of both their bodies, the new bruises on mine.

I wake up and go on another Tinder date with a different guy. It's so awesome. Right away we're talking about trauma and tenderness and obfuscation. Healing in relationship. Growth. Authenticity. We end with a warm hug, mildly sexy. I'm leaving tomorrow but I wanna see him some more. I get to Jade's and text new guy, *hey, you could come cuddle with me under the stars. And I would like it*. Bryan is his name, and I tell Jade he's not like anyone I've met before. Several hours pass and then he texts back: *Awesome, no thanks*. Fine. I take a walk and read a poem and feel fine. It's dark and I'm sitting across from Jade when she looks up and says, *Bryan texted me. I considered not telling you but*. She has that frowny look she gets when she's dismayed with something on my behalf. We made a bunch of the same matches this week and he was one of them. It doesn't hurt my feelings but it does. He says *sorry, I guess I was still in my polyamorous mindset*. Three texts later he says, *sorry, I was just sending good vibes to new friends, not hitting on her*. Now we have a word for this kind of man.

I think about writing my story; all the pieces are there. Are all the pieces there? And then I think, *what the fuck can I write about them?* I realize I gotta write a story about *me*, figure out why the fuck I'm attracted to them, not try to figure out why they are the way they are, what they want, what they mean, why violence and vulnerability gets everything all twisted. I'm tired of all this figuring. So instead, I'll write a story with just the facts, and the only facts about feelings that I really know are the ones that happen inside me. Maybe *I'm* the problem. Maybe *I'm* trying to avoid something by seeking intimacy with people I've just met. And violence. But it just happens that way and I can't help but be honest about the way I see them and love them instantly sometimes. And how I want them to hurt me.

I go home and I dream of The Motel. I register, wander around the pool and see some familiar faces from Tinder, but I haven't chosen yet. I lose my keys and my phone and after I've climbed three flights of filthy stairs to get to my room, I open the door and find someone else in there. I'm pissed and I go back down to say I'm leaving. As soon as I find my keys. This is the same motel in all my dreams. It looks different and different things happen there but it's The Motel. I don't know what it means.

When I wake, I see that The Poet has texted me. It's been two weeks of silence. He says, *wanna make out again? Without all the loving stuff right away?* I read it again and again. I screenshot it for Jade. She says, *omg are u dead?* I say yes, *I'm texting u from my coffin.* I don't know how to answer him. I tell Jade I don't know how to answer him. *Right away*, he said. *Loving stuff*, he said. I think of all the goddamn fucking time Jade and I spend parsing male communications.

Finally I text him, *I don't know how to an-*

swer. He says *ok*. I want to, but I don't feel normal about him. He knows this. It's the reason he refused to see me and stopped talking to me. Because I said *I'm already in love with you*. And this did not please him or fit with his situation. He can make out with his girlfriend. He can make out with his various regular sex partners. He could walk out his door and make out with any woman on the street. Jade says, *the fact that he texted you speaks for itself* and I agree.

I think about how it would feel to see him and touch him again. I know the way it would feel would be exactly what we both want but that…for some reason, I am not allowed to say that. We can do it, but I can't say it. So, fuck that. I text him, *I think I'd rather get to know you and be friends, if you're interested. Without too much touching. Because touching …idk I just lose my mind, in general but especially with you*. It would be hard to be friends, but easier than not seeing him. I don't really give a fuck about fucking; I want to *know* him.

He doesn't reply. I try another way. I type, *here's a story about me*, and send him a story about me. 20-year-old me treading the abyss. I don't feel that far away from her, but I know more now. I think he'll find it relatable. He doesn't reply. I'm pissed and I *miss* him. One day, two days, no reply.

I tell my therapist about it and the healthy way I responded to his tempting invitation. She's the one who taught me about how touch fucks me up and always cautions me to be careful about it. She congratulates me on my reply and worries about the glitter on my eyes. I tell her I scheduled a date with a more available poet who is brilliant and kind and hasn't caused me to see stars or want to text him compulsively. We are enthusiastic about my healthy choice. I forget to tell her about me getting violently fucked by a stranger on purpose the other day.

Lately when I touch myself, it's different. It's not that I'm imagining The Poet's perfect hands on me or fantasizing about him. It's that my body feels altered since he touched me, and now when I touch myself, it feels his absence. Or something. It feels good to touch myself and I like my body under my hands but the curve of my hip craves the alchemy that happens under *his* hands, looking in *his* eyes, the impossible sensation of being both in and outside of my body, the sensation of being *more*. It's not even sexual. I hate to say it but it's....spiritual.

I think of the wound my ex-husband opened up in me, the closest I can come to recalling a similar experience. How the magic was instantaneous and then he opened a place inside me. I didn't know he was a predator though. So he opened the place in me and planted something there. Something that still lives in my body. This is the demon that loves being down in my parents' basement, on certain winding roads, in the shadows of tall pines. I know The Poet has a lil demon on his shoulder, but it's not that kind. Fourteen years later this thing still lives inside me. And it still pains me. I remember the moment exactly, lying in bed with my husband seeing me and touching me and how he opened me up. The exact place on my left side, inside my belly...and stars poured out.

I don't believe in any of this shit, these are metaphors obviously. I left off *spirituality* some time ago, though the signs of it are still written on my body. I don't believe in demons but there's no other word for this thing that gnaws at me. Opening, planting, wound, soul, demon, stars. I don't have words for it. It is a real thing that lives inside my body that can sometimes be prayed into submission but never yet has been prayed away.

Before the Big Tinder started kissing me on the couch, he looked at the Virgin on my shoulder and asked if I'm religious. I said, *no, but I dig Mary. The story, you know?* I hesitated and considered and I knew it would take too long and that I would probably cry if I tried to tell about her and doubted he would give a shit anyway but before I could not say it he said, *kiss me*, and I did.

The Virgin though. For some reason, right after I got sober I was reading a lot of Thomas Merton. And my friend was into this painter, also a monk, who painted these icons, mostly Mary. Between the icons and the Merton, I started seeing something in her. Something I could pray to, and I did. The Woman Clothed With The Sun. Which is, after all, a star. How the thing about her is how her purity lets the light shine *through* her unsullied.

Last month, after the Magic Hour, after we'd said goodbye, I reported to Jade right away. A couple of minutes later he texted, *send me a screenshot of the text you just sent your friend*. I got a little shock and looked over my shoulder. Then I remembered I had just told him that I tell her everything and then I laughed and then I took the screenshot and sent it to him. The report said:

> *Oooh*
> *My god*
> *Five stars*
> *Ten stars*
> *Five hundred stars oh my god*

Rilke's always going on about stars. What do they mean? How to explain what happened in that Hour without becoming a terrible gross cliche or lying completely? *"World was in the face of the beloved..."* Universes poured forth from inside me and him, full of stars. Infinity opened up and flowed between us in some sweet calm familiar way. Falling into each other's faces and there was a whole world in there. Jade and I have been calling it *faceworld*, though we both think that's a stupid name. She knew right away what I was talking about when I tried to explain. She said, *it is not for words*. I remember seeing god one time when I was high on meth and I kept trying to say it to someone in riddles and paradoxes, the only way it would come out of my mouth. God was a shape like a star or a flower or a flower made of stars all moving, made of movement, golden if it had a color.

There's one of those inside me, and for some reason, it's part of the one inside him and we stood there looking at each other's faces in, and of, that golden flow. I don't know how to say it. But it doesn't matter because anything I try to say about it means he does not want to see me again. Maybe I am remembering it wrong. Maybe I'm making it all up, like a story. Maybe The Poet is, in fact, a real Bryan. Whatever he is, he is not a predator. I know that much.

While I'm touching myself into this terrible awareness of his absence, I get the idea to make a video of myself masturbating to send to him. Sex is a language I am allowed to speak to him. Sex is safe. I look in the mirror. I've forgotten my phone and abruptly I think *fuck him anyway*. I watch my face, but my reflection is cold and hard and I can't see any stars in it. My own face is impenetrable to me. How can this be?

There are stars and there are stars. Rating stars. The stars you see when it's a little more than light choking. Starry eyes. Heavenly bodies. The sun. The stars you see when your husband punches you unexpectedly in the face. Stars in your belly, like butterflies but made of fire. Rilke's stars, sometimes stone inside you.

We are made of light, I guess that's what I'm trying to say.

After the fucking, the big man built for violence walked me to my car and I looked at the sky. Mountain dark. So many stars. I stood there staring up. He said *you wanna see something cool? Wait thirty seconds. Wait one minute.* I was surprised, because he had seemed eager for me to leave. He went back into his place. While I waited, I wondered is he lonely. I wondered was his scar worth it. I wondered why I can't help but want to clean other people's wounds, and being a little hurt when they won't let me. He came back and said, *don't drop them*, and handed me night vision glasses. *Look at the sky*, he said. *Look at me*, he said. I looked at the sky. I looked at him. I *oooh*ed and *ahhh*ed and he grinned like a little kid. While I looked at everything and remembered it is all made of light, he said, *sometimes I just sit alone and look at the night with these* and I said, *yes*.

Yes. Why would you ever do anything else?

Left

It arrives in my body unbidden: a trajectory towards the earth, the half-corpse left behind. I'm not here or there, not now or then. I am always being murdered, and not in a metaphorical transformation sort of way.

I try to put it in a poem. That only makes it worse.

I climb into bed beside him. I can't reach for him. I can't speak, though things are dire. He's half asleep. I can't think what would wake me, what would shake me from this trajectory. I can't think.

Now-me makes words out of then-me's scream.

No-one can hear me.

Places I Have Lived and the Colors of Them

My mother,
Denver:
shadow.

The house on Xavier,
Denver:
white.

The yellow house,
Cushing:
yellow.

A grey house beside a pond,
Stillwater:
cattail.

The duplex outside of town,
>Payne County:
>>red.

A white house with red trim,
>Stillwater:
>>turtle.

A pale brown house against a hill,
>Cimarron:
>>horny toad and wild marigold.

The house where Stevie dropped a brick on a mouse,
>Miami:
>>blue, grey.

A yellow house with a circus for no audience,
>Mosquero:
>>yellow and cut pine.

The white house on Jefferson Street,
>Clayton:
>>ice, sunset, crab apple, tarpaper.

The house I couldn't believe they'd buy,
Cimarron:
mint green, salmon, deerflesh.

Libby's house,
Miami:
white and goathorn.

The house on Duck Street,
Stillwater:
black.

The house in Pawnee,
Pawnee:
black.

The house I couldn't believe they bought,
Cimarron:
black.

Libby's house,
Miami:
bumblebee.

A yellow house,
Springer:
milkwhite and shadow, pink.

By now in the list I'm very tired. I am 16.
The rest of it is harder to say. I don't know
why.
After now I live in my own places, alone with
my son, except when I don't.

Public housing,
Springer:
sand, brown, purple, black and white.

Arrott House student family apartments,
Las Vegas,
orange and green.

The adobe with the bad water,
Las Vegas:
mud and silvergold.

The blue apartment on Lincoln,
Las Vegas:
blue, maroon, gold.

A white duplex with orange trim,
Las Vegas:
black, silver, red.

My mother's trailer,
Pecos:
night.

Gregg House student family apartments,
Las Vegas:
orange.

A cold blue two story,
Romeroville:
rabbit and pinon.

A warm brick two story,
Las Vegas:
silver and black.

The house where Fat Kitty died,
Cushing:
white, amber, lime.

Duplex,
Stillwater:
teal, plaid, shadow.

My mother's house,
Payne County:
white.

Billy's house,
Las Vegas:
blue.

The house on Lincoln, Las Vegas:
mirror
The Mists of Avalon, Trade paperback:
steelblue and mirror
New Mexico State Hospital, Las Vegas:
grey pine mirror

Stepmother's house,
  Denver:
  brick.

The place in the canyon,
  Gilpin County:
  snow, pine, bear.

Shannon's house,
  Arvada:
  teal and red.

Jolie's house,
  Arvada:
  white.

The condo on Quail Street,
  Wheat Ridge:
  skyblue

Children's Hospital,
  Aurora:
  silver, milkwhite

The condo on Quail Street,
Wheat Ridge:
pink

Mariposa apartments,
Taos:
green, adobe, gold

Stepmother's house,
Denver:
green, brick, grey

Your face,

Everywhere:

all of them.

Myself,

Here:

milkthistle

moon

sunlight

Self Titled

I've never been in a real swamp
I think of this because I am thinking about how much she waters she waters and waters and waters so I am thinking it's got to be getting like a swamp under there

And then to myself I say hey how would you know you've never been in one

well I've got this song stuck in my head

It doesn't sound like it did when I started listening to it all the time last week when I was swimming in him and he's gone whoever he was I barely remember but the song just stays on in there

Someone else wrote me a poem about soothing shame with violence
Someone else wrote me a story about flying away

and then I ask myself what is it you're trying to say no one wrote anything for you and she is not your mother nothing is wrong

Self, I say
We're doing fine
And if you wanna cry, cry
If it's just an eyelash or a little piece of dirt fine
It's the wind
It's cut onions
It's not your husband
It couldn't be you never were
Married but you're not now are you
So it couldn't be your husband you don't have one
Self you didn't die we're doing fine it doesn't matter
Husband is not a person who kills you so it's not that

You never had one

Sweetheart you're doing fine and in the morning we'll check the garden

We'll dig down and see if it's a swamp under there we'll dig something up to prove she should lighten up on the water just let the sun catch up a little just let those little onions grow it's not like every time you smell one it feels like you might be murdered soon
you didn't die you're doing fine

If one year from April to September you cut onions every night into a certain size always doing it wrong and then you didn't die that wouldn't be something to hurt you all over inside fourteen years later the smell of onions wouldn't matter and we know the difference don't we between then and now we know the difference between these little onions growing up and ones cut a certain size we'd know a murderer we'd know a husband we know the difference we know how much water is too much whether or not we ever went to a real swamp and

baby, we're doing *fine*

Nicole Morning is a librarian and the author of *Soft Animal*, *Tinderness*, *Maximum Fancy*, *n*, and *A Thing That Happened in 2020*. She edits the ongoing zine series *Basia Mille*. Her writing has appeared in *Nudie Magazine*, *Horror Sleaze Trash*, and Hello America audio compilations.

Nicole's zine *Tinderness* was awarded Best Litzine at Canzine 2020.

Her most recent release is an audio recording of *Soft Animal*, available from Hello America Stereo Cassette.

nicolemorning.com.

OTHER VERY FINE TITLES FROM
TRIDENT PRESS

Blood-Soaked Buddha/Hard Earth Pascal
by Noah Cicero

it gets cold
by j avery

Major Diamonds Nights & Knives
by Katie Foster

Cactus
by Nathaniel Kennon Perkins

*Sixty Tattoos I Secretly
Gave Myself at Work*
by Tanner Ballengee

The Pocket Peter Kropotkin

The Pocket Emma Goldman

The Silence is the Noise
by Bart Schaneman

The Pocket Aleister Crowley

Los Espiritus
by Josh Hyde

Propaganda of the Deed:
The Pocket Alexander Berkman

The Soul of Man Under Socialism
by Oscar Wilde

The Pocket Austin Osman Spare

America At Play
by Mathias Svalina

With a Difference
by Francis Daulerio and Nick Gregorio

Western Erotica Ho
by Bram Riddlebarger

Las Vegas Bootlegger
by Noah Cicero

The Green and the Gold
by Bart Schaneman

www.ingramcontent.com/pod-product-compliance
Lightning Source LLC
Chambersburg PA
CBHW022010120526
44592CB00034B/768